PRESENTING THE PAST · TOPICS
TUDOR
SEAFARERS

Shaan Butters

Oxford University Press 1989

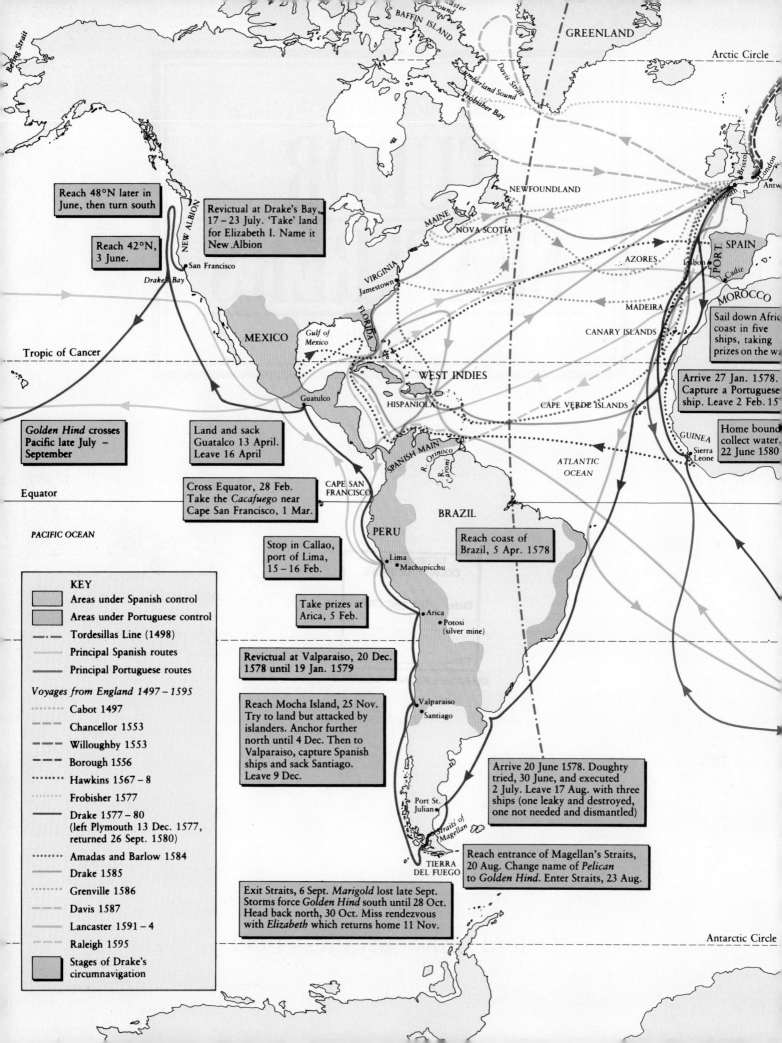

Reach 48°N later in June, then turn south

Reach 42°N, 3 June.

Revictual at Drake's Bay, 17–23 July. 'Take' land for Elizabeth I. Name it New Albion

Golden Hind crosses Pacific late July – September

Land and sack Guatalco 13 April. Leave 16 April

Cross Equator, 28 Feb. Take the *Cacafuego* near Cape San Francisco, 1 Mar.

Stop in Callao, port of Lima, 15–16 Feb.

Take prizes at Arica, 5 Feb.

Reach coast of Brazil, 5 Apr. 1578

Revictual at Valparaiso, 20 Dec. 1578 until 19 Jan. 1579

Reach Mocha Island, 25 Nov. Try to land but attacked by islanders. Anchor further north until 4 Dec. Then to Valparaiso, capture Spanish ships and sack Santiago. Leave 9 Dec.

Arrive 20 June 1578. Doughty tried, 30 June, and executed 2 July. Leave 17 Aug. with three ships (one leaky and destroyed, one not needed and dismantled)

Reach entrance of Magellan's Straits, 20 Aug. Change name of *Pelican* to *Golden Hind*. Enter Straits, 23 Aug.

Exit Straits, 6 Sept. *Marigold* lost late Sept. Storms force *Golden Hind* south until 28 Oct. Head back north, 30 Oct. Miss rendezvous with *Elizabeth* which returns home 11 Nov.

Sail down Afric[a] coast in five ships, taking prizes on the wa[y]

Arrive 27 Jan. 1578. Capture a Portugues[e] ship. Leave 2 Feb. 15[78]

Home bound collect water. 22 June 1580

KEY

Areas under Spanish control
Areas under Portuguese control

– · – Tordesillas Line (1498)
Principal Spanish routes
Principal Portuguese routes

Voyages from England 1497–1595

········· Cabot 1497
– – – – Chancellor 1553
– – – Willoughby 1553
– – – Borough 1556
········· Hawkins 1567–8
········· Frobisher 1577
———— Drake 1577–80 (left Plymouth 13 Dec. 1577, returned 26 Sept. 1580)
········· Amadas and Barlow 1584
———— Drake 1585
········· Grenville 1586
········· Davis 1587
– – – Lancaster 1591–4
········· Raleigh 1595

Stages of Drake's circumnavigation

GREENLAND
Arctic Circle
BAFFIN ISLAND
Davis Strait
Cumberland Sound
Frobisher Bay
NEWFOUNDLAND
MAINE
NOVA SCOTIA
VIRGINIA
Jamestown
FLORIDA
Gulf of Mexico
MEXICO
San Francisco
Drake's Bay
NEW ALBION
Tropic of Cancer
Guatulco
WEST INDIES
HISPANIOLA
SPANISH MAIN
CAPE SAN FRANCISCO
Equator
PACIFIC OCEAN
PERU
Lima
Machupicchu
Arica
Potosi (silver mine)
BRAZIL
R. Orinoco
R. Caroni
ATLANTIC OCEAN
Valparaiso
Santiago
Port St. Julian
Straits of Magellan
TIERRA DEL FUEGO
Antarctic Circle
SPAIN
PORT.
Lisbon
Cadiz
MOROCCO
AZORES
MADEIRA
CANARY ISLANDS
CAPE VERDE ISLANDS
GUINEA
Sierra Leone
Plymouth
Bristol
London
Antw[erp]
Bering Strait

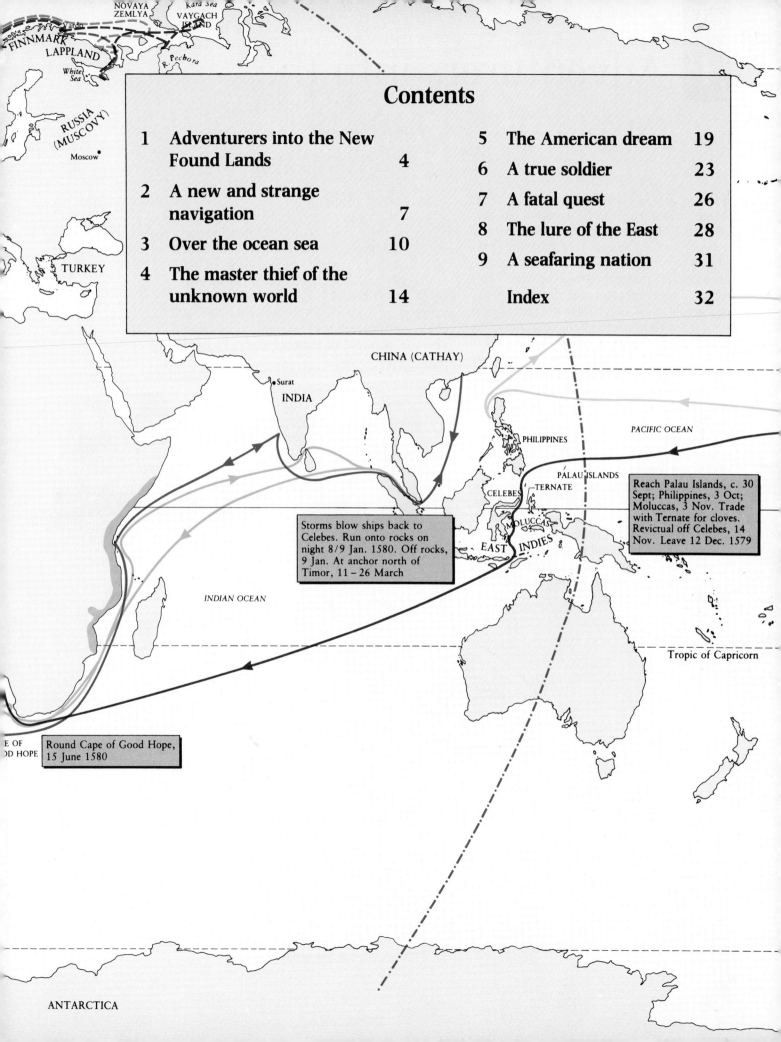

Contents

Storms blow ships back to Celebes. Run onto rocks on night 8/9 Jan. 1580. Off rocks, 9 Jan. At anchor north of Timor, 11–26 March

Reach Palau Islands, c. 30 Sept; Philippines, 3 Oct; Moluccas, 3 Nov. Trade with Ternate for cloves. Revictual off Celebes, 14 Nov. Leave 12 Dec. 1579

Round Cape of Good Hope, 15 June 1580

1 Adventurers into the New Found Lands

In the early Middle Ages, some scholars believed the earth to be a round, flat disc, surrounded by sea. People thought that if you went too far west, or east, you would fall off the edge of the world. By the fifteenth century, most scholars understood that the world was a sphere, and that if you sailed west far enough, you would eventually reach the East. People still did not know about all the countries of the world. World maps showed only Europe, North Africa and part of Asia. It took courage to explore further afield. But during the fifteenth century European seamen, mainly from Spain and Portugal, made many voyages of discovery.

The map below shows the 'Old World': the continents of Asia, Africa and Europe. This was the known world before Christopher Columbus found out about America. Asia was seen as the source of gold, spices and fabulous riches. Columbus thought he could reach it directly by sailing west; he didn't realise America was in the way. When he found America, he thought it was part of Asia. Later, people realised America was a fourth continent, a 'New World'.

God, gain and glory

What led these voyagers to risk their lives at sea? Bernal Diaz, the Spanish adventurer, said, 'We came here to serve God, and also to get rich'. Explorers could serve God by converting heathens to Christianity, and get rich through trade, or plunder (violently robbing ships or cities), or discovering a gold mine. They could also win personal or national glory. Richard

In Cabot's day Arab, Italian and Portuguese merchants brought spices to Europe. Cabot wanted to bypass these merchants and bring spices directly from Asia, to sell them in Europe at a good profit.

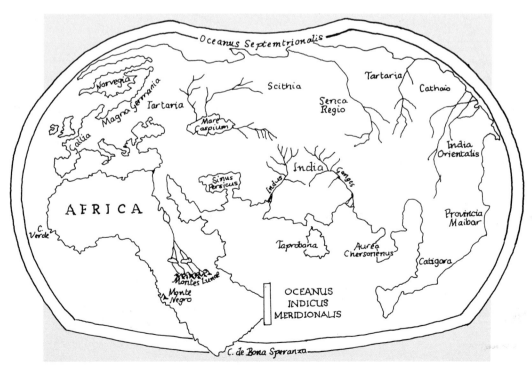

A world map by the German, Henricus Martellus, printed c.1489. ('c.1489' means 'approximately 1489'; 'c.' is short for 'circa', the Latin for 'about'.)

It was in a small ship, possibly like this, that Cabot crossed the Atlantic. Conditions on board were cramped and uncomfortable. The men usually slept on deck. Food sometimes ran out on long voyages, and water went foul. Lack of fresh fruit (containing vitamin 'C') often led to scurvy, a disease from which many sailors died.

Hakluyt the Younger, writing in the 1580s about English explorers, said:

66 Some seek authority and places of commandment, others experience by seeing of the world, the most part worldly gain, and the fewest number the glory of God and the saving of the souls of the poor and blinded infidels (unbelievers; non-Christians). 99

Many explorers sought a sea-route to Asia, the source of luxury goods like spices, which were much in demand in Europe. Most Europeans had a boring diet and wanted spices (like pepper, nutmeg, cloves and cinnamon) to vary it. Also, without refrigerators it was hard to keep food fresh. Spices were useful to hide the taste of bad meat!

By 1498 the Portuguese had found an eastern route, round Africa. Columbus, seeking a western route, had discovered the West Indies and part of South America for Spain. In 1498, the Pope defined the Tordesillas line. Spain and Portugal agreed not to interfere in each other's business on either side of this line.

John Cabot, the 'Great Admiral'

English seamen joined in the voyages of discovery in Henry VII's reign (1485–1509). Several expeditions left from Bristol, a proud and busy port. A Bristol chronicle records for 1497:

66 The land of America was found by the Merchants of Bristol in a ship of Bristol, called the *Mathew*. 99

This expedition was led by an Italian, John Cabot. He had read the writings of Marco Polo, who in the 1270s travelled eastwards overland to the empire of Cathay (China). Cabot wanted to see for himself the magnificent Chinese cities described by Polo, but he hoped to reach them by sailing west, across the Atlantic. He came to England and won Henry VII's support. Bristol merchants supplied money and the ship. In 1497 Cabot set sail for America with 20 men. The journey to North America took over a month. Captains lacked accurate maps and navigational instruments, and sailing ships were at the mercy of the weather. Going to sea was a dangerous business.

We don't know exactly where Cabot went, but he explored somewhere along the northeast coast of America (see map, pages 2–3), in the region of Maine, Nova Scotia or Newfoundland. Cabot himself thought this was Asia. A Venetian, Lorenzo Pasqualigo, wrote in 1497:

66 (Cabot) has come back and says he has discovered mainland 700 leagues (2100 miles) away, which is the country of the Grand Khan (ruler of China), and that he coasted it for 300 leagues and landed and did not see any person. 99

John Day, an English merchant, said in a letter probably written to Columbus in 1497–8:

66 They disembarked there ... and they found tall trees of the kind masts are made. All along the coast they found many fish. 99

These are sixteenth century pictures of sea monsters. Some are exaggerated or imaginary, but many people believed in them and sailors sometimes reported sighting some very strange creatures at sea!

On his return, Cabot became famous. Pasqualigo wrote: 'He is called the Great Admiral and vast honour is paid to him'. But in 1498 Cabot set out on another voyage and never returned.

From Bristol to 'Brasil'

Even before Cabot, it is possible that Bristol merchants may have discovered North America. In a letter John Day suggests that Bristol men found a land which they first thought was an island called 'Brasil', but which they now believed to be Cabot's mainland. 'Brasil' was not the South American country we know today, but an imaginary island placed in the Atlantic by fifteenth century cartographers. Day gives no date for the Bristol discovery, but voyages seeking 'Brasil' left Bristol in 1481 and in the early 1490s, so it might have been then.

Bristol men accompanied Cabot, and in the early sixteenth century continued to sail to North America. Robert Fabyan's chronicle for 1501–2 tells us:

66 This year also were brought unto the
king three men, taken in the new found
Island. These were clothed in beasts'
skins, and ate raw flesh, and spoke
such speech that no man could
understand them. 99

One group of Bristol merchants, formed in 1502, was soon called the 'Company Adventurers into the New Found Lands'.

But from now until 1550 there were only a few more voyages of discovery and some trading expeditions to the New World (see page 10). There was no need to go far afield, as English trade with Europe prospered. Also Henry VIII did not want to offend Spain and Portugal by challenging them overseas. English enterprise had to wait.

1 a) How many miles are there in a league?
b) Compare Martellus's map of 1489 with the modern map at the front of the book. List the differences between them.

2 a) Explain in your own words why Hakluyt thought men went on voyages of discovery. Which does he think is the most common motive? Which motive do you think he approved of most? Give the reasons for your choice. b) What were John Cabot's reasons for going on his voyage?

3 a) What hints are there in John Day and Lorenzo Pasqualigo's accounts of Cabot's voyage that he had not in fact reached Cathay? b) How could the new land still be of value to England?

4 Where were the Bristol men's 'Brasil' and 'New Found Lands'?

A new and strange navigation

This is how some sixteenth century cartographers imagined the Arctic: the North Pole surrounded by an ocean, divided into channels by land masses. Many writers did not think that cold and ice would pose too big a problem for sailors. There was therefore thought to be a choice of sea routes to Asia over and around the top of the earth.

By 1550, Portugal dominated the south-eastern sea route to Asia, and Spain dominated the south-western one (round America and across the Pacific). Both countries claimed control of trade within 'their' overseas areas. After the Reformation, when England turned Protestant, England's relations with Catholic Portugal and Spain became difficult. Some English merchants now began to think it might be sensible to find their own trade routes and passage to Asia, outside the areas of Spanish and Portuguese control. In 1548 Edward VI's government invited John Cabot's son, Sebastian, to England to help with this. He was a respected geographer and had previously been working for the Spanish government.

The way of the North

It seemed obvious for England to avoid the Spanish and Portuguese by seeking a northern passage. Already under Henry VIII (1509–47) a merchant called Robert Thorne had suggested 'the way of the North'. In 1527 he had written:

66 If from the said new found land (North America) the sea be navigable, there is no doubt, but sailing northward and passing the Pole, descending to the equinoctial line (Equator), we shall hit these islands (East Indies), and it should be a much shorter way, than either the

7

Spaniards or Portuguese have. I judge, there is no land uninhabitable, nor sea unnavigable. 🙮

Many geographers believed that there were not only sea passages to southern Asia across the Polar sea, but also longer routes round the north-west of America and round the north-east of Europe and Asia (see map, page 7).

In 1550 a fall in demand for cloth, England's main export to Europe, made the matter urgent. Clement Adams, a teacher, reported:

🙮 At what time our Merchants perceived the commodities of England to be in small request with the countries about us certain grave Citizens of London resolved upon a new and strange Navigation (voyage) for the search of the Northern part of the world, to open a passage to our men. 🙮

The government decided to seek the north-eastern route to Asia, believing it would pass well populated areas of the cold North that would want England's woollen cloth.

To the land of the midnight sun

The north-east passage expedition set out in May 1553 with three ships and 95 men. It was led by a soldier, Sir Hugh Willoughby, and by Richard Chancellor, an expert navigator. As the expedition left England, Clement Adams reported:

🙮 (Many sailors) looked oftentimes back, and could not refrain from tears. (Chancellor) left behind him his two little sons, which were in the case of orphans if he sped not well. 🙮

They sailed up the Norwegian coast, making for Vardo in Finnmark (see map, pages 2–3). A storm separated them, and only Chancellor reached Vardo. Willoughby's ship and the third ship lost their way. In September they reached Arzina, in Lappland. Willoughby's journal tells us the weather was so bad already that they decided not to try to set out to sea again, but to spend the winter where they were. They sent out search parties, but saw no signs of human life. The cold was terrible and in the end all 70 men died. Russian fishermen found their frozen bodies when summer came.

Chancellor was luckier. After Vardo, says Adams, Chancellor took his ship and crew:

🙮 towards that unknown part of the world, and sailed so far, that he came at last to the place where he found no night at all, but a continual light and brightness of the sun shining clearly upon the huge and mighty Sea. 🙮

In August, Chancellor reached the White Sea and landed. Fishermen told him he was in a country called Russia, or Muscovy. He then journeyed overland, by sled, to Moscow. Here, the Russian Tsar (Emperor), Ivan IV, received him in friendship and permitted trade. In 1554 Chancellor returned safely home. But only two years later he died on his way back from another trip to Muscovy. His sons were, after all, left fatherless.

Above: Chancellor described the Tsar's palace as 'a fair Castle, the walls whereof are of brick, and very high ... wherein are nine fair Churches'. St Basil's is shown here. The Tsar, Ivan IV (inset), 'wore an imperial crown upon his head, and a staff of crystal and gold in his right hand'.

Below: The Arctic, where temperatures sometimes drop below −40°C.

A 'Iodia', or Russian fishing boat. It has oars as well as sails. Stephen Borough met many Russian Iodias and fishermen in 1556.

Today there are few whales left because people have hunted and killed so many of them. Many people think whales should be protected. But Borough's men saw them only as a danger. One day, says Borough, 'there was a monstrous Whale ... so near to our side that we might have thrust a sword ... in him, which we durst not do for fear he should have overthrown our ship ... but God be thanked, we were quietly delivered of him.'

The Muscovy Company

Chancellor had not discovered a 'new' land but he did start a friendship between Russia and England. In 1555 Queen Mary (1553–8) officially recognized the Muscovy Company, giving it a monopoly (sole control) of all trade and discovery in the North. Sebastian Cabot was its Governor. A small but useful trade developed: English cloth was exchanged for Russian wax, flax, tallow, cables and ropes.

Terrible abundance of ice

The north-east passage to Asia was not discovered. In 1556 the Muscovy Company sent Stephen Borough to find it in a ship called *Searchthrift*. He sailed north east of the White Sea, to Novaya Zemlya, the Kara Strait and Vaygach Island (see map, pages 2–3). Borough recorded meeting a Russian fisherman:

66 whose name was Gabriel, who showed me very much friendship, and he declared unto me, that all they were fishing for Salmons and Morses (walruses). 99

Gabriel showed Borough the way to the River Pechora. Another fisherman, Loshak, went on shore with Borough at Vaygach Island and showed him the bloodstained idols worshipped by the local people, the Samoyeds.

Borough was much hindered by conditions in those Arctic seas. Much of the Arctic Ocean is permanently frozen. Some parts are only ice-covered in winter, but in summer even these may be treacherous with ice floes and bergs. In the end the *Searchthrift* had to turn back because, Burough said, 'of great and terrible abundance of ice'. Arthur Pet and Charles Jackman tried again for the Company in 1580. They reached the Kara Sea, but ice forced them, too, to retreat, and Jackman's ship was lost. Not till 1879 did a (Swedish) ship sail through the north-east passage.

1 Explain the difference between the polar route suggested by Thorne, and the north-east passage route attempted by Willoughby and Chancellor. What did Thorne believe to be the advantages of the polar route?

2 Why did Edward VI's government decide to attempt a) a northern route in general, and b) the north-east route in particular?

3 Was Thorne right that northern seas were navigable? Give reasons for your answer.

4 Why do you think some of Willoughby and Chancellor's sailors wept as they left England? Write a list of a) the achievements and benefits of Willoughby and Chancellor's expedition, and b) the unfortunate side of it. On balance, do you think the expedition was worth making?

3 Over the ocean sea

Not everyone sought a northern passage to Asia, or tried to avoid the Spanish and Portuguese. A few bold merchants risked trading directly with Africa, hoping for pepper, gold and ivory, or with the New World, hoping for silver, sugar or pearls. One of these was John Hawkins.

John Hawkins, slave trader

John Hawkins (1532–95), one of the greatest seamen of Elizabeth I's reign (1558–1603), came from a Plymouth merchant family. His father, William, had traded with Africa and Brazil in 1530–2. John wanted to trade with the West Indies. In 1559 he moved to London to raise money for his journey. He made his first transatlantic voyage in 1562 (see maps, pages 2–3 and below). An anonymous account published by Hakluyt explains his plan:

66 Master John Hawkins, having made diverse voyages to the isle of the Canaries and there by his good and upright dealings being grown in love and favour with the people, informed himself amongst them of the state of the West Indies. And being assured that the negroes (native black Africans) were very good merchandise in Hispaniola (now Haiti and the Dominican Republic), and that store of negroes might easily be had upon the coast of Guinea, resolved with himself to make trial thereof. 99

Most Europeans, like Hawkins's Englishmen, had never seen black people before they visited Africa. Some of them felt respect for the power of the African rulers. Others were afraid, either because black skins seemed strange to them, or because of the fighting skills of black warriors. Others looked down on some of the black people as 'savages', maybe because they wore few or no clothes, or did not have such technically developed tools or weapons (like guns) as the Europeans. But most seem simply to have felt wonder at seeing people and ways of life different from their own.

In ancient times slavery was common. By 1500 it was rare in Europe, but still common in Africa and in Arab countries. African and Arab rulers enslaved their prisoners of war; Moslem pirates carried European Christians into slavery; the Turks bought slaves from Africa.

John Hawkins's voyages to the West Indies. The third voyage was disastrous. Only two out of nine ships returned home. Many men died and some were captured by the Spanish and tortured or put into slavery. Hawkins survived and went on to fight against the Spanish Armada.

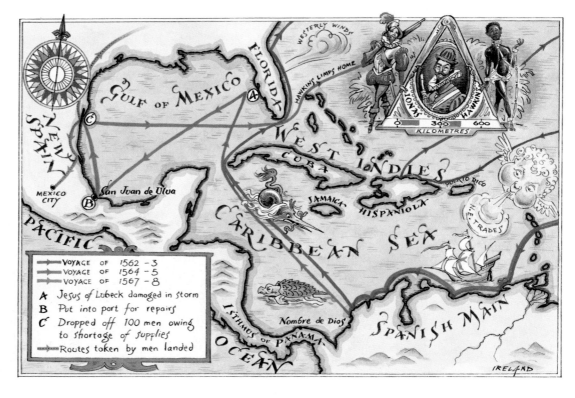

VOYAGE OF 1562 – 3
VOYAGE OF 1564 – 5
VOYAGE OF 1567 – 8
A Jesus of Lubeck damaged in storm
B Put into port for repairs
C Dropped off 100 men owing to shortage of supplies
Routes taken by men landed

Black Africans were used as slaves in the mines and plantations of the Spanish New World. Slaves were unfree. They were owned by a master and had to obey him. They were bought and sold like animals. Slaves were often treated cruelly, and forced to work long and hard in harsh and dangerous conditions. At first, the Spanish settlers had used the native Indians to work the West Indian mines. But the Indians died in their thousands of overwork and ill treatment. So the Spanish imported African slaves instead. Thousands of these died too, but the Europeans were able to go on buying or capturing more from Africa. Many English and European merchants made rich profits from this terrible trade in human beings. Conditions on board the slave ships were often appalling. The slaves were packed close together and chained up below deck, and many died of disease before they reached their destination. Some churchmen attacked the slave trade as inhuman, and some merchants refused to take part. But most people accepted it, and either did not know, did not think or did not care about the sufferings of the slaves.

A risky game

Spanish colonists were often willing to trade with foreign merchants because Spain could not supply enough slaves. Hawkins probably

Above: John Hawkins aged 48. According to a Spaniard: 'He is such a man as that any man talking with him hath no power to deny him anything he doth request.' People also remarked on his self control, a rare characteristic in the sixteenth century. Hawkins was also unusual in taking care of his men; he avoided overcrowding his ships so there was better hygiene and less sickness. In 1592 he founded a home for old mariners (seamen: sailors) in Chatham.

Left: Sixteenth century Africa was the home of many different tribes (peoples) and civilizations (ways of life), and of several great kingdoms under powerful rulers. Some of the peoples lived in impressive walled cities, others in small villages. This map from the period shows some of these features.

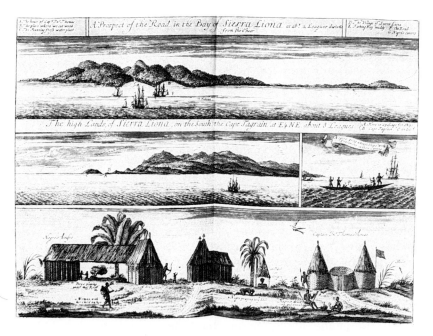

hoped for peaceful trade, but the plan was risky. A treaty of 1489 allowed English merchants to trade directly with the Spanish Canary Islands, but Spain only allowed foreigners to trade with the New World if they were Catholic, and sailed via Spain and with Spain's permission. Hawkins was Protestant, and had no Spanish licence. Portugal tried to stop all other nations trading with Africa. Hawkins was living dangerously, but he was lucky. In Guinea:

> 66he got into his possession partly by the sword and partly by other means, to the number of 300 negroes at the least, besides other merchandises. With this prey he sailed over the Ocean Sea (Atlantic) unto the island of Hispaniola where he had peaceable traffic [and sold his negroes in return for] hides, ginger, sugars and pearls.99

The voyage was described as a 'prosperous success'.

Hawkins's second voyage, in 1564, (see map, page 10) was also successful. This expedition had Queen Elizabeth's support and included a royal ship; Elizabeth wanted to encourage English overseas trade. But Philip II of Spain was furious. Relations between Protestant England and Catholic Spain now worsened.

Above: Hawkins took slaves in Africa either by attacking Africans directly or getting them from Portuguese traders. In 1567 he joined in an African war with the King of Sierra Leone, who promised Hawkins any prisoners as slaves. This drawing was made long after Hawkins's time, but gives a good idea of what he would have seen in Africa.

Below: A slave market in Algiers. Hawkins started England's involvement in the slave trade. In the eighteenth century, Britain became the main European nation to trade in black African slaves. At last people realised the slave trade was evil. Britain banned it in 1807, and abolished slavery throughout the British empire in 1833.

A troublesome voyage

Hawkins made what he called his 'third troublesome voyage' in 1567 (see maps, pages 2–3 and 10). This time, the Spanish colonists feared Philip II's anger and were less willing to trade. Then, near Florida, one of the Queen's ships, the *Jesus of Lubeck*, was damaged in a storm. Hawkins had to anchor in the port of San Juan de Ulua, Mexico, for repairs.

Suddenly, a large Spanish fleet arrived to take the New World silver (page 15) back to Spain. Hawkins dared not give reason for war by keeping the Spaniards out, for Elizabeth still wanted peace. Both sides promised good behaviour, and the Spaniards entered the port. But once in, they plotted a surprise attack. At about 10 am on 23 September, 300 Spaniards attacked one of Hawkins's ships, the *Minion*. Battle raged till nightfall. During the fight, a sailor on the *Jesus*, Job Hortop, tells how Hawkins asked his page, Samuel, for a cup of beer, cheered up his soldiers and persuaded the gunners to stand by their ordnance (cannons). When he put the cup down, a cannon ball blew it away:

66 which nothing dismayed our General, for he ceased not to encourage us, saying, 'Fear nothing, for God, who hath preserved me from this shot will also deliver us from these traitors and villains'. 99

Only two out of nine ships escaped. The *Judith* went on ahead, and Hawkins limped home later in the *Minion*. It was a terrible journey. Hortop said:

66 Victuals were so scarce that we were driven to eat hides, cats, rats, parrots, monkeys and dogs. 99

Only a handful of the *Minion*'s 200 men survived.

Many of Hawkins's Protestant sailors were captured after San Juan and imprisoned by the Spanish Inquisition, a Catholic organization dedicated to stamping out heresy (religious 'errors'). Some were tortured. A few were burnt at the stake. Others were flogged or, like Job Hortop, sent as slaves to row in the galleys (warships with oars). Here, said Hortop,

66 we were chained four and four together. Our lodgings was on the bare boards. Hunger, thirst, cold and (whip) stripes we lacked none. 99

Hortop escaped in 1590, after 22 years.

Against Spain

After the Spaniards' treachery (breaking their promise) at San Juan, most Englishmen abandoned peaceful trade with the New World and saw Spain as the enemy. From 1577 Hawkins was Treasurer of the Navy, and was busy improving the Queen's ships, ready for war. He replaced or rebuilt as many ships as possible. The new style ships were lower, smaller, faster and stronger, more suitable for the high seas.

During the Armada campaign, 1588 (see p. 18), Hawkins fought bravely and earned a knighthood. He died on his last voyage, a West Indian raid with Drake (see page 18), in 1595. It failed, and one of Hawkins's captains, John Troughton, thought Hawkins died of grief at letting the Queen down. On his deathbed, Hawkins told Troughton

66 to acquaint Your Highness (Elizabeth) with his loyal service and good meaning towards Your Majesty, even to his last breathing. 99

The *Jesus of Lubeck* was an old warship of Henry VIII's reign. It sailed with Hawkins in 1567. Big ships like this, with high overhanging 'castles' at either end, were suitable for home waters, but not strong enough for ocean sailing.

1 a) What do you think Hawkins's general motives were for making his voyages?
b) Explain in your own words Hawkins's specific plan for his 1562 voyage. c) Describe where Hawkins went on each trip.

2 a) Why was it safe for Hawkins to trade with the Canaries, but risky in Africa and the New World? b) What sort of treatment could an English Protestant expect if he was captured abroad by the Spanish?

3 a) Why were Africans wanted as slaves in America? b) What did people think about the slave trade in the sixteenth century? What do you think of it?

4 The master thief of the unknown world

Above right: Sir Francis Drake by Nicholas Hilliard.

Right: The Isthmus of Panama, showing where Sir Francis Drake attempted to steal Spanish gold and silver.

Hawkins had hoped for peaceful trade with Spain's New World. But by the 1570s Protestant adventurers saw Catholic Spain as the enemy. They tried to plunder Spanish ships and towns overseas. These plunderers were called pirates or privateers. Privateers had government permission to attack a hostile country's ships. Pirates were unlicensed sea-robbers.

One of England's most famous pirates was Francis Drake (c.1542–1596). John Stow, an Elizabethan chronicler, described him as:

> 66 more skilful in all points of navigation that any ever was, he was also of perfect memory, great observation, eloquent, skilful in artillery. In his imperfections he was ambitious for honour, unconstant in friendship, greatly desirous of popularity. 99

Others called him arrogant and boastful.

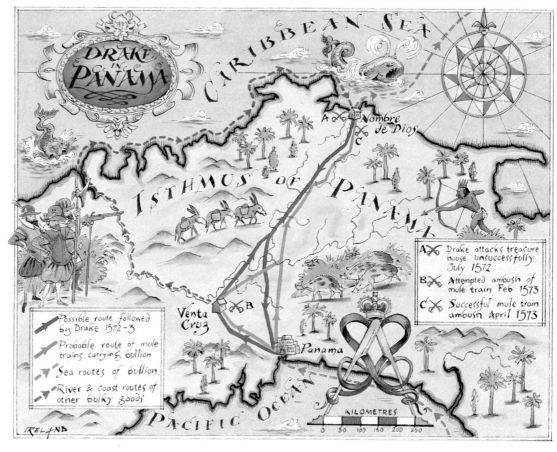

DRAKE IN PANAMA

CARIBBEAN SEA

Nombre de Dios

ISTHMUS OF PANAMA

Venta Cruz

Panama

PACIFIC OCEAN

A ✕ Drake attacks treasure house unsuccessfully July 1572
B ✕ Attempted ambush of mule train Feb 1573
C ✕ Successful mule train ambush April 1573

→ Possible route followed by Drake 1572-3
→ Probable route of mule trains carrying bullion
→ Sea routes of bullion
→ River & coast routes of other bulky goods

KILOMETRES
0 50 100 150 200 250

IRELAND

In 1549, Catholic violence forced Drake's Protestant family to flee from its Devon farm. Drake grew up in poverty on a Thames river boat. He became a skilled sailor. In the 1560s he sailed to America and back with his relative, John Hawkins.

Drake fought at San Juan de Ulua (see page 13). He already disliked Spaniards because they were Catholics; now he saw them as personal enemies. For revenge, and to get rich, Drake turned pirate and plundered Spain's ships. Then, he decided to raid Spain's New World treasure houses.

The raid on Panama

Spain owned fabulous gold and silver mines in Peru. The treasure was packed onto mules, and slaves guided the mule-trains across the mountainous Isthmus of Panama to Nombre de Dios (see map, left). Here, the treasure was stored in treasure houses until a Spanish fleet arrived to ship it home.

In 1572, Drake took two ships and 73 men to Panama. *Sir Francis Drake Revived*, published in 1626, describes his adventures. (Extracts in this section are taken from it.) It was compiled in about 1592 to win Queen Elizabeth's support and is biased in Drake's favour, but Spanish documents confirm most of it.

Drake made three attempts to steal Spain's treasure. First, he attacked the treasure house at Nombre de Dios:

66 We were at the town by three of the clock after midnight. The town took alarm, the soldiers and inhabitants presented us with a jolly hot volley of shot. 99

After a fierce fight, Drake was shot in the leg. He tried to keep going, but eventually:

66 ... his fainting against his will betrayed it (the pain); the blood having first filled the very prints which our footsteps made. 99

Later he tried again. Guided by the Cimaroons, black slaves who had escaped their Spanish masters, he crossed the Isthmus:

66 Every day we were marching by sunrising; we continued till ten in the forenoon, then resting till past twelve, we marched till four, and then by some river's side we reposed ourselves. 99

Then he tried to ambush a mule train near Panama. His men hid on either side of the road but one of them was drunk and careless. He stood up to see who he could hear riding past. A Spanish horseman saw him and galloped off to warn the mule train. The ambush failed, but Drake refused to give up. He marched back to Nombre de Dios.

66 There came three mule trains, one of fifty mules, the other two of seventy, every of which carried three hundred pound weight of silver. These were guarded with forty-five soldiers which caused some exchange of bullets and arrows. But in the end these soldiers thought it the best way to leave their mules with us. 99

Drake captured £20,000 of treasure (worth about £20 million today). He returned to Plymouth a rich man. But about 40 of his men had died.

A secret voyage

Drake's next plan was to explore the Pacific. In 1572 he'd glimpsed it from a tree-top on the Isthmus of Panama, and had prayed God 'to give him life and leave to sail once in an English ship in that sea'.

Queen Elizabeth, who feared upsetting Spain, would not agree until 1577, when relations with Spain were bad anyway. But the voyage's aims were still kept secret to avoid alerting or further upsetting Spain. We don't know Drake's exact orders, but they were probably to sail through the Straits of Magellan to explore the Pacific coast of South America. The idea would have been to trade and look for areas to settle, before returning through the Straits again. Drake doubtless hoped for plunder.

In the Panama raid of 1572, people called the Cimaroons were a great help in guiding Drake's men in a foreign country. It would have been difficult for Drake and his men to find their way through the dense vegetation shown in this modern photograph of Panama.

Five ships and 164 men left Plymouth in December, 1577. Drake himself commanded the *Pelican*, later renamed the *Golden Hind* after the emblem of one of his backers, Sir Christopher Hatton. The main map (p. 2–3) shows Drake's route. He captured Portuguese ships off Africa, and then crossed the Atlantic.

Mutiny aboard?

But there was trouble on board, involving Drake's former friend, Sir Thomas Doughty. We don't know exactly what happened. An anonymous account published by Hakluyt says that Doughty's actions were 'tending rather to contention (argument) or mutiny (revolt against authority)', but gives no details. A narrative called *The World Encompassed* (encircled), compiled in 1628 by Drake's nephew, talks vaguely of 'mischief' and 'plots' against Drake. But the account of one of Drake's sailors, John Cooke, says that Drake put Doughty in charge of a captured Portuguese ship, containing chests of valuables. Cooke relates that Doughty caught Drake's brother, Thomas, in the act of breaking open the chest. Doughty told Drake, who:

66 presently falling into some rages seemed to wonder what Thomas Doughty should mean to accuse his brother and did assure himself that he meant to shout at his reputation. From this time forth grudges did seem to grow between them. 99

Drake had Doughty beheaded at Port St Julian in July, 1578.

Into the South Sea

Later that summer, Drake sailed through the Straits of Magellan into the South Sea. In *The World Encompassed* it says this ocean was called the Mare (sea) Pacificum (peaceful) by some, but seemed to be more of a Mare Furiosum (furious). Terrible storms caused the loss of one ship, the *Marigold*, while another, the *Elizabeth*, returned home.

Drake escaped from the storms 'as it were through the needle's eye'. When they subsided, he explored up the west coast of South America. In 1579 he continued north, plundering Spanish ships and settlements. Some Spaniards captured by Drake have left us accounts of life on board. At meals, Drake was served on silver plates with gold borders, while music was played in the background. He conducted Protestant services on deck morning and evening. (Several other English seamen of the period did this, including John Hawkins.) Two Spaniards wrote very differently about Drake's relationship with his crew:

66 He treats them with affection, and they treat him with respect. He shows them great favour, but punishes the least fault. All said that they adored him. 99

66 All his men tremble before him. 99

Across the Pacific

Drake's plundering brought him £140 000 of silver (worth about £140 million today). Now he had achieved his aim and planned to go home. He decided to avoid Magellan's Straits, for fear of Spanish attacks. Instead, he sought the west end of the north-west passage (see

This drawing of 1603 shows the *Golden Hind* attacking a Spanish ship, nicknamed the *Cacafuego* (Spitfire) near Lima in 1579. Drake plundered as many Spanish and Portuguese ships as he could during his voyage, seizing their rich cargoes, but usually showing mercy to the captains and crews. The *Golden Hind* was described by a sixteenth century eye-witness as 'very stout and very strong'. Until recently a replica of the *Golden Hind* could be seen at Brixham, Devon, but it sank in 1987.

Caca Fogo.　　　Caca Plata.

TYPVS ORBIS TERRARVM.

QVID EI POTEST VIDERI MAGNVM IN REBVS HVMANIS, CVI AETERNITAS OMNIS, TOTIVSQVE MVNDI NOTA SIT MAGNITVDO. CICERO:

p. 28), but couldn't find it. He reached latitude 48° North in June 1579, and cold then drove him south down the Californian coast. He landed, probably at or near a place now called Drake's Bay, north of San Francisco. He called the country 'New Albion' (New Britain), taking possession of it for the Queen. The native Indians who lived there thought these strange intruders must be gods and offered sacrifices to Drake and his men.

In July:

66 our general now considering that the extremity of the cold cut off all hope of finding a passage through these northern parts, thought it necessary to lose no time: and therefore with general consent of all, bent his course directly to run with the Islands of the Moluccas. And so having nothing in our view but air and sea, without sight of any land for the space of full 68 days together, we continued our course through the main ocean. 99
(*The World Encompassed*, 1628)

Above: Compare this sixteenth century map by Henricus Ortelius with the modern map at the front of the book. Notice the land south of Magellan's Straits: Terra Australis Incognita (the unknown Southern Land). People thought that there was a vast undiscovered continent here, rich in gold, 'wherein many strange monsters lived'. Drake couldn't find any such land, and concluded it didn't exist. Was he right?

Below: Part of Drake's Bay, California. Drake 'set up a monument of our being there, ... namely, a plate of brass fast nailed to a post', recording that he took possession of the land in Elizabeth I's name.

Against the Armada

Drake was Vice-Admiral of the Fleet in 1588. There is a story that he heard of the Armada's approach while playing a game of bowls on Plymouth Hoe, and said, 'There's time to finish the game and beat the Spaniards too'. But this remark is first mentioned in the eighteenth century, so it was probably made up. (Can you think why?) Drake then played a gallant part in the Armada campaign.

The end of the game

But afterwards the glory faded. Drake's raid on Lisbon (then ruled by Spain) failed dismally; it was badly organized and about 11 000 men died of disease. Finally, Drake and Hawkins failed in their attack on the West Indies in 1595. Drake died at sea, of yellow fever, in 1596.

To his own and future ages, Drake became a legend. He was the Protestant hero who challenged the might of Catholic Spain. But not everyone approved. To some, as the chronicler Stow tells us, he was simply a successful pirate, 'the master thief of the unknown world'.

1 Why did Drake dislike a) Catholics b) Spaniards?

2 a) Why is it hard to be sure what happened in the Doughty affair? b) Do you think Doughty was guilty of mutiny? Give your reasons.

3 Do you think Drake was a good commander? Give reasons. Would you have liked to serve under him? Say why (or why not).

4 List the differences between: a) the modern world map (p. 2–3) and Ortelius's map (p. 17) b) Ortelius's map and Martellus's map on page 4. c) Is Ortelius's map more accurate than Martellus's?

5 a) Drake's Log Book for the voyage round the world is lost. Use the map on pages 2 and 3 to draw up your own Log Book (a list of when and where the ship sailed, and what happened, in order) for the *Golden Hind*'s journey. b) Why did Drake become a national hero?

6 How did Drake behave when he was wounded at Nombre de Dios? What does this tell you about his character?

Drake proudly displayed his coat of arms, the sign of a gentleman, seen here on a drum kept at Buckland Abbey in Devon. Drake was not born a gentleman, but the wealth he gained from piracy enabled him to buy a gentleman's house. He bought Buckland Abbey from Sir Richard Grenville in 1580, for £3,400.

Drake arrived in the Moluccas in November, 1579. Here, he traded and bought cloves. In January, 1580, the *Golden Hind* narrowly missed being shipwrecked on a rock. Then Drake sailed on westwards. In September, about 100 weary men came home to Plymouth.

Drake returned, said the chronicler Camden, 'abounding with riches, but more illustrious and exceeding in glory'. He had circumnavigated (sailed round) the world. He was the first leader of an expedition to do so. (Magellan's expedition, 1519–22, made the first successful circumnavigation, but Magellan himself was killed during it.) Even a Spanish nobleman, captured by Drake, called him 'one of the greatest mariners that sailed the seas, both as a navigator and a commander'.

Elizabeth knighted Drake in 1581. Nor were his days of glory over. In 1585, when war broke out between England and Spain, he attacked the West Indies successfully. In 1587 he made a daring raid on Cadiz harbour and 'singed the King of Spain's beard' by damaging with fire part of the great Armada (fleet) which Philip II was building to invade England.

5 The American dream

During Elizabeth I's reign, some people thought that England should build her own empire abroad to rival Spain's. John Dee, magician and scientist, made up the term 'British Empire'. He thought Britain had the right to rule North America because he believed the legend that a Welsh prince, Owen Madoc, had founded colonies there in about 1170. The two Richard Hakluyts (see page 31) thought that England should be allowed to rule North America because John Cabot had discovered it for Henry VII. They wanted Englishmen to set up colonies in America, to farm, fish, trade and build houses. Such colonies could supply England with useful produce and be markets for English industrial goods.

In the 1580s, when England and Spain were close to war, a courtier called Walter Raleigh (see p. 26) took up the idea of colonies. He wanted to set up a North American colony which could also be a base for attacking the Spanish West Indies. In 1584 Raleigh sent his servants, Philip Amadas and Arthur Barlow, to find a suitable site north of Florida. Barlow wrote an account of the voyage which Hakluyt the Younger published in *Principal Navigations* in 1589, to encourage further colonization.

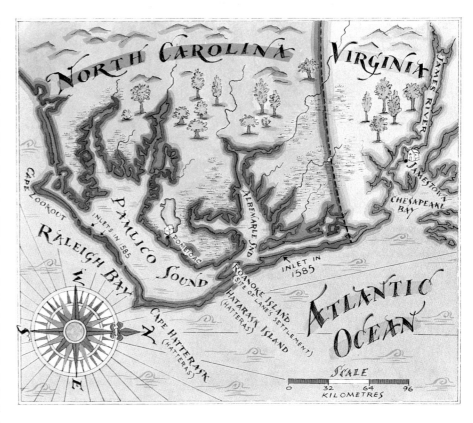

Valleys filled with cedar trees

Amadas and Barlow sailed via the West Indies to the Carolina Banks (see above map, right). They landed on Hatarask Island. Here:

66 Under the bank or hill, whereon we stood, we beheld the valleys filled with goodly Cedar trees, and having discharged our arquebus (gun) shot, such a flock of Cranes (the most part white) arose under us, with such a cry redoubled by many Echoes, as if an army of men had shouted altogether. 99

After a few days they met the native Indians: 'very handsome, and goodly people, and in their behaviour as mannerly, and civil, as any of Europe'. The king, Wingina, had been wounded fighting in a continuing war with neighbouring peoples. Amadas and Barlow made friends with the king's brother, who was named Granganimeo. They met his wife, who:

66 was very well favoured (pretty), of mean stature (short), and very bashful. In her ears she had bracelets of pearls, hanging down to her middle and those were of the bigness of good peas. 99

Soon the English visited Granganimeo's village, on Roanoke Island. The men were away, but Granganimeo's wife welcomed them. Yet when some Indian warriors returned, armed, from hunting, Barlow's men reached for their weapons. They wouldn't risk staying the night.

The Golden Age recovered

The expedition returned to England. Barlow's account portrays America as a land flowing with milk and honey:

66 The earth bringeth forth all things in abundance, as in the first creation, without toil or labour. We found the people most gentle, loving, and faithful, void of all guile (without deceit), and treason, and such as lived after the manner of the golden age. 99

Part of the Virginia coastline. The Carolina Banks were a barrier of narrow, sandy islands off the east coast of North America. Wind and tides have eroded and added to these islands, changing their shape, so those of today are different from those of the 1580s.

19

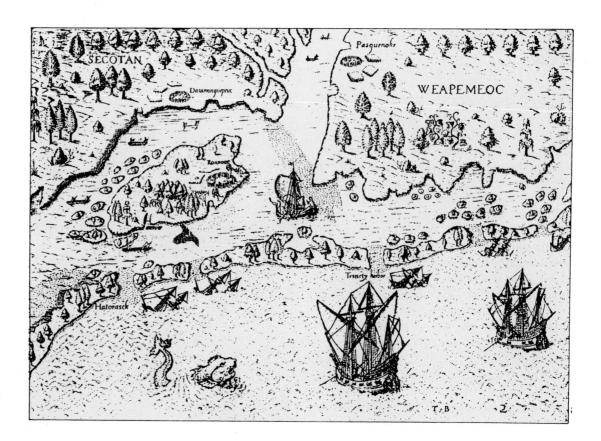

Theodore de Bry's engraving of a drawing by John White showing the arrival of the English in Virginia.

(It was thought that when the world was first created, there was a 'Golden Age' of leisure, happiness and plenty.) Barlow didn't mention an incident which an English sailor reported in 1586: that the expedition made a first landing south of Hatarask, where the 'Wild Indians ate thirty-eight Englishmen'.

The first colony in Virginia

In 1585 Raleigh sent a second expedition, with Sir Richard Grenville (see page 23) in charge, to set up a colony in the Roanoke area, now called Virginia in honour of Elizabeth, the Virgin Queen. Raleigh hoped Virginia would be profitable for England to trade with. Thomas Hariot, a scientist on the expedition, listed Virginia's produce: pearls; grapes (for wine); fur and skins, iron; flax and hemp (for cloth and rope); pitch and tar (for waterproofing); wood, such as cedar (for ships, houses and furniture); walnuts (for oil); Indian corn, or maize; fruits; fish; meat; tobacco.

Grenville organized the first English colony in America, 'appointing Master Ralph Lane ... General of those English (about 100) which were to remain there' (*Holinshed's Chronicle*). Grenville explored the mainland, and got permission from Wingina to settle the north-west end of Roanoke Island. Then he went home to organize food supplies. Lane built a fort and explored the area further. Thomas Hariot studied the Indian language and customs. John White, an artist, painted pictures of native life. Hariot thought that though the Indians:

66 have no such tools, nor any such crafts, sciences and arts as we; yet in those things they do, they show excellency of wit (intelligence). If means of good government be used, they may in short time be brought to civilization, and the embracing of true religion. 99

The Indians, for their part, viewed the English and their religion with awe. Hariot wrote that some people could not decide whether the Englishmen were gods or men.

But things soon went wrong. The colonists had brought food from England, but by the spring of 1586 stores ran low, and still Grenville's supplies didn't come. The English had no seed to grow corn, and lacked the skill to build fish traps. At first the Indians gave them food willingly, but later they grew hostile as their own supplies dwindled. Finally, colonists and Indians fought each other, and Wingina was killed. In June the colonists came home. Two colonies were set up on Roanoke in 1586 and 1587, but both failed.

The towne of Pomeiock and true forme of their howses, couered
and enclosed some wth matts, and some wth barcks of trees. All compassed
abowt wth smale poles stock thick together in stedd of a wall.

Above: This is John White's drawing of the Indian village of Pomeiooc. Granganimeo's village on Roanoke probably looked like this.

Below left: White's drawing of an Indian woman and young girl. Notice the little girl's doll. Hariot said the children were 'greatly delighted with puppets (dolls) brought out of England'.

Below right: White's drawing of an Indian brave in war paint. Barlow reported that Indian weapons were 'bows and arrows, and swords made of wood, bones, animal teeth and shells'. Hariot said that they had 'no edge tools or weapons of iron or steel; neither know they how to make any.'

Top: This engraving by Theodor de Bry (from a lost drawing by White) shows Indians making canoes. Barlow wrote: 'They burn down some great tree. They set fire into it, and when it hath burnt it hollow, they cut out the charcoal with their shells, and by this means they fashion very fine boats, and such as will transport twenty men'.

Above: This is John White's drawing of Indians fishing. Hariot said the Indians had two fishing methods: 'the one is by a kind of weir (fish trap) made of reeds. The other way is with poles made sharp at one end, by shooting them into the fish' from a boat or while wading in shallow water.

21

and by wars. But for the most part they died of mere famine. There were never Englishmen left in a foreign country in such misery as we were in this new discovered Virginia. 🙦

But enough people stuck it out, and with tough leadership the colony survived. Then John Rolfe, one of the colonists, managed after much experiment to produce a tobacco that people in England liked. (Indian tobacco was too bitter for them.) Smoking had already reached England, but Raleigh's colonists made it more popular. It was probably they who introduced clay pipes into England, shaped like the Indian pipes, with long stem and bowl. (Real Indian pipes, however, were often made of stone.) So the Jamestown colonists already had a market in England for their tobacco. By the late 1620s the tobacco trade flourished, and the colony prospered.

A dream come true?

Around Jamestown grew England's first overseas empire, and later the United States of America. For the English, the dream of colonies came true. But, as European settlements in America spread, so the native Indians lost their lands. Their way of life was gradually stamped out. Eventually most of them were killed. So, tragically for them, the Indian fear recorded by Hariot was finally fulfilled.

🙦 Some would prophesy that there were more of our generation yet to come, to kill theirs and take their place. 🙦

1 a) Where was i) Raleigh's Virginia?
  ii) Jamestown? Why were they so named?
  b) Why did Englishmen want to found a colony in North America?

2 Show where Barlow's account of Virginia is misleading. Why should this be so?

3 a) Give some examples of Indian skills.
  b) How did Hariot view the Indians? Comment on his attitude.

4 a) How well prepared for colonial life were Lane's men? b) Why did Lane's colony at Roanoke fail?

5 a) Do you think the Jamestown settlers had learnt any useful lessons from what happened at Roanoke? Give reasons.
  b) Why did the Jamestown colony eventually survive and prosper?

The Indians grew tobacco plants. 'The leaves thereof being dried and brought into a powder,' wrote Hariot, 'they use to take the smoke thereof by sucking it through pipes made of clay, into their stomach and head.' He thought tobacco smoking prevented illness, whereas today we know it causes diseases like lung cancer.

Jamestown, Virginia

In 1606 a company of London merchants organized another expedition which founded a new colony on the James River in 1607. It was called Jamestown (see map, pp. 2–3 and 19), in honour of England's new king, James I (1603–25). In some ways Jamestown was a good site: it had a good harbour and was easy to defend. But it was marshy and unhealthy, and men soon fell ill. As at Roanoke, the colonists relied mainly on supplies from England and corn from the Indians to survive. At first they did not really try to grow their own everyday food. This was partly because many of the colonists were gentlemen, and not used to hard labour. It was also because the colonists wanted to get rich quickly: they preferred to look for gold mines, or experiment with special crops, like sugar cane, which might bring them big profits through trade. As a result they came close to starving.

A hard start

The colonists suffered terribly for the first few years, and many people died. One account says:

🙦 Our men were destroyed with cruel diseases as swellings, burning fevers,

6 A true soldier

It became quite fashionable under Elizabeth for gentlemen to dream up plans for expeditions overseas. One of the most heroic gentleman adventurers was Sir Richard Grenville, though he is remembered more for the way he met his death than for what he did during most of his life! Grenville (c.1542–1591) came from an old West Country family. He was a proud man, and hoped to win honour and glory by his deeds. He followed a career as a soldier in the 1560s and then grew interested in overseas discovery.

Right: Sir Richard Grenville, painted in 1571. Grenville sailed in 1591 with Lord Thomas Howard, intending to prevent Spanish treasure fleets from the West Indies from reaching Spain.

Dreams of the South

In 1573–4, just after Drake's raid on Panama, Grenville asked royal permission for a voyage for the:

66 discovery of all lands southward beyond the equinoctial (Equator) and which lands be not already possessed by any Christian prince (to) advance the honour of our sovereign Lady and Country, with enlarging the bounds of Christian religion, and the beneficial utterance (exporting) of the commodities of England. 99

He may have planned to colonize the southern area of South America, or possibly to seek 'Terra Australis' (see page 17).

The Queen seemed to accept the plan, and Grenville started his preparations. But in 1574–5 Elizabeth was on better terms with Spain than she had been earlier. She didn't want a voyage which might involve plundering Spain's New World and thereby spoil relations between England and Spain. At the last minute, she forbade Grenville to go. When relations with Spain were bad again, 1576–7, it was Drake who was given command of an expedition to South America (see page 15). Grenville must have been very disappointed.

The Roanoke connection

Grenville got his chance to go to sea in 1585, when he led an expedition to Virginia (see page 20), to set up a colony for Raleigh. You may remember that he soon came back to England to fetch supplies for the colonists.

Grenville returned to Roanoke in 1586. But he arrived in July, just too late to save the colony, which Lane's men had abandoned in June. Then Grenville:

66 unwilling to lose the possession of the country, determined to leave some men behind to retain possession. Whereupon he landed fifteen men in the Isle of Roanoke, furnished plentifully with provisions for two years. 99

He himself came home. The fifteen colonists were driven away by hostile Indians, and never heard of again.

Danger in the Azores

So far, Grenville hadn't had much success. But he still hoped to do something memorable. In 1591, during the war against Spain, Grenville was Vice-Admiral in a fleet led by Lord Thomas Howard. They sailed to the Azores, planning to ambush the Spanish treasure fleet on its return from America (pp. 14 and 15). But the treasure fleet didn't arrive. After some months, many sailors fell sick. The English went ashore on the Island of Flores to rummage (clean) the ships.

Suddenly, 55 Spanish warships under Don Alonso de Bazan appeared. Howard was taken by surprise. He only had 22 ships, and these were not ready to fight. They were still being cleaned; some of the sailors were on shore finding fresh food and water; and anyway half the men were too ill to be useful. So Howard ordered the fleet to flee.

Raleigh (who was not present) later wrote the 'official' account of what happened. The Spanish fleet came upon the English one so quickly that

66 our ships had scarce time to weigh their anchors, but some of them were driven to let slip their anchor cables and set sail. 99

Grenville, in the *Revenge*, waited to pick up the men who were ashore. He was therefore slow to follow Howard and missed the wind. He could have fled in the other direction.

66 But Sir Richard utterly refused to turn from the enemy, alleging that he would rather choose to die than to dishonour himself, his country, and Her Majesty's ship. 99

The last fight of the *Revenge*

So Grenville stayed and fought, hopelessly outnumbered. The Spaniards tried to board the *Revenge*, but, according to Raleigh, were beaten off again and again:

Reconstruction of a sixteenth century galleon. Rubbish and sewage were often thrown below deck and left to mix with the ballast (sand, gravel or stones used to keep a ship stable in the water). When a ship was finally cleaned, the crew threw away the old ballast. They scrubbed the ship out and disinfected it with vinegar. Then they took clean ballast on board.

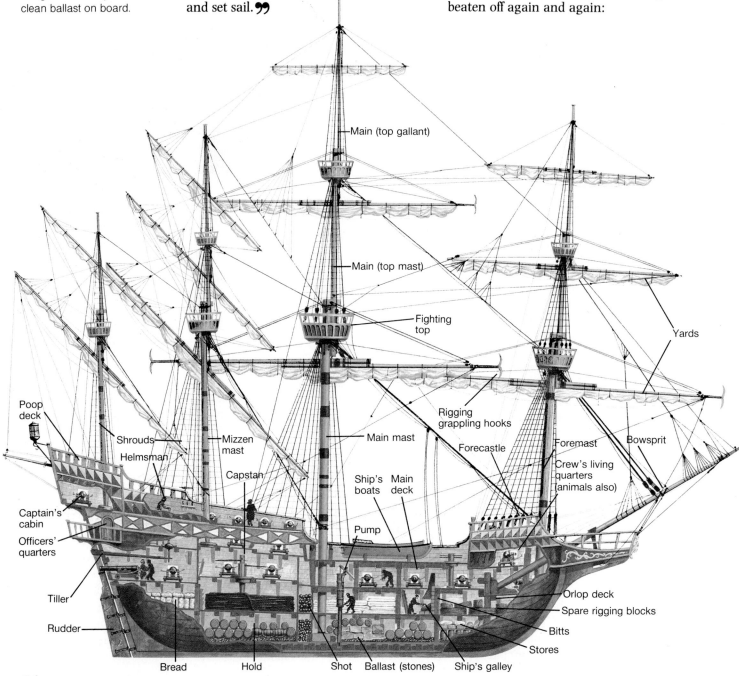

Main (top gallant)

Main (top mast)

Fighting top

Yards

Poop deck

Shrouds

Helmsman

Mizzen mast

Capstan

Main mast

Ship's boats

Main deck

Rigging grappling hooks

Forecastle

Foremast

Bowsprit

Crew's living quarters (animals also)

Captain's cabin

Officers' quarters

Pump

Tiller

Rudder

Orlop deck

Spare rigging blocks

Bitts

Stores

Bread

Hold

Shot

Ballast (stones)

Ship's galley

> "Yet, as the Spanish ships were wounded and beaten off, so always others came in their place, the *Revenge* having never less than two mighty galleons at once by her side."

The *Revenge*'s last fight began at 3 pm and continued into the evening. At 11 pm, Grenville:

> "being shot into the body with a musket as he was a dressing, was again shot in the head. All the gunpowder of the Revenge was now spent, all her pikes broken, forty of her best men slain, and the most part of the rest hurt."

The Spaniards were still well supplied. Grenville realized that there was little hope for the *Revenge* and commanded that the ship be sunk rather than be surrendered to the Spaniards. But the exhausted crew wanted to surrender. Grenville, mortally wounded, at last lost heart. By now:

> "... the ship was marvellous unsavoury, filled with blood and bodies of dead and wounded men like a slaughterhouse."

Grenville surrendered. He died soon afterwards.

Raleigh's official verdict was that Grenville 'ended his life honourably in respect of the reputation won to his nation'. Grenville would have been pleased with this. After a lifetime of failure he had died a hero's death. A Dutch traveller in the Azores, Linschoten, said his last words were:

> "Here die I, Richard Grenville, with a joyful and quiet mind, for that I have ended my life as a true soldier ought to do, that hath fought for his country, Queen, religion and honour."

1 Using the evidence in this chapter and chapter 5, explain where you a) approve, and b) disapprove of how Grenville handled the 1585 Virginia expedition.

2 Why did Grenville sail to the Azores in 1591?

3 a) Why do you think Elizabeth's government wanted an 'official' account of the Battle of Flores published? b) How far do you think we should trust Raleigh's account?

4 a) What conduct would Grenville have thought to be 'dishonourable' at Flores? b) Why did he die content? c) Do you agree with his actions at Flores? Explain why, or why not?

Above: The last fight of the *Revenge*.

Left: 'I saw the dolphin chase the flying fish', wrote young Philip Gawdy, who sailed with Grenville in 1591 for a taste of adventure. In his letters home he mentioned the 'great kindness I find at Sir Richard's hands', and said proudly, 'I am become a reasonable good mariner.' Imprisoned for ransom after the battle of Flores, Gawdy was released in 1592 and reached home safely.

7 A fatal quest

Above: Sir Walter Raleigh (or Ralegh) by Nicholas Hilliard. The Elizabethans probably pronounced his name 'Rawley'.

Below: Raleigh's exploits in Guiana in search of El Dorado.

We have already met Sir Walter Raleigh (c.1552–1618) as the promoter of the Roanoke voyages (see page 19). He became Queen Elizabeth's favourite in 1581. As Elizabeth liked to have him at court, he couldn't lead overseas expeditions himself. But in 1592 he fell from favour after a secret love affair with one of the Queen's ladies, Elizabeth Throckmorton, whom he then married. No longer required at court, he was now able to go adventuring.

The legend of El Dorado

In 1595 he set off for Guiana, in South America (see map below). He wanted to find the lost Inca empire of El Dorado. The Spaniards had already destroyed the native Inca civilization of Peru. But according to legend, one Inca Prince and his followers fled east and founded a second Inca empire somewhere in South America. It was fabulously wealthy in gold and ruled by El Dorado. One Spanish tale which Raleigh reported was that:

66 at the times of their solemn feasts, when the Emperor carouseth (drinks) with his captains, certain servants of the Emperor, having prepared gold made into fine powder, blow it through hollow canes upon their naked bodies, until they be all shining from the foot to the head. Upon this sight, and for the abundance of gold in the city, the Spaniards called it El Dorado. 99

El Dorado, meaning 'Golden One', was applied first to the Emperor, then to the country and capital city. The Spaniards thought the capital city, Manoa, lay up the Orinoco River, in Guiana. Some claimed to have visited Manoa, but no one knew exactly where it was. To this day, no one has ever found it.

Spain claimed that Guiana was part of her empire, though it wasn't fully under Spanish control. Raleigh hoped that soon England could defeat the Spaniards in Guiana, win over the native Indians, and establish an English empire.

Voyage to Guiana, 1595

Raleigh described his expedition in an account published in 1596. It was written to persuade the government to pay for further expeditions to Guiana. He wrote:

66 On Thursday the 6th of February, in the year 1595, we departed England.... We arrived at Trinidad the 22nd of March 99

(see map, left). Here they made friends with the Indians, who lamented that the Spaniards had made slaves of the Indian people and their rulers. Raleigh then sacked a Spanish settlement and captured its Spanish governor.

Raleigh told the Indians that he had been sent by a great Queen to free them from the cruel rule of the Spaniards.

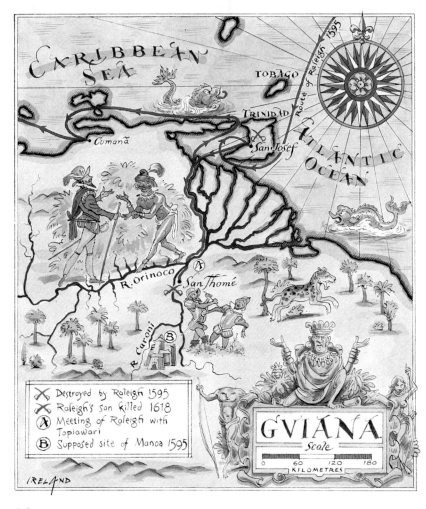

CARIBBEAN SEA

TOBAGO

TRINIDAD

ATLANTIC OCEAN

·Cumaná

San Josef

R. Orinoco

San Thomé

R. Coroni

✗ Destroyed by Raleigh 1595
✗ Raleigh's son killed 1618
Ⓐ Meeting of Raleigh with Topiawari
Ⓑ Supposed site of Manoa 1595

GVIANA
Scale
0   60   120   180
KILOMETRES

IRELAND

A hard journey

Then Raleigh crossed to the mainland and journeyed up the Orinoco. He and his men travelled in a few small boats. Everyone was packed close together on the hard boards. There was no shelter. According to Raleigh:

> 66 there was never any prison in England more unsavoury, especially to myself, who had before been cared for in a sort far more differing. 99

After about 20 days, Raleigh's men reached the River Caroni. Here an Indian lord, Topiawari, told them that:

> 66 in his father's lifetime there came down into Guiana a nation from so far off as the sun slept, with so great a multitude as they could not be resisted, and that they were called the Epuremei and had slain so many of the ancient people as there were leaves in the wood upon all the trees, and had now made themselves lords of all, and had built a great town and that their houses have many rooms. 99

Hoping this was El Dorado's empire, Raleigh tried to explore up the Caroni. But the river was too swollen with rain, and he gave up. Instead, the party explored the area on foot. Raleigh wrote:

> 66 I never saw a more beautiful country ... every stone that we stooped to take up promised either gold or silver. 99

They all then returned safely to England. There Raleigh wrote enthusiastically of Guiana. Men would:

> 66 find there more rich and beautiful cities, more temples adorned with golden images, more sepulchres (tombs) filled with treasure than Pizarro found in Peru. Whatsoever prince shall possess it, shall be lord of more gold than the King of Spain. 99

Elizabeth wasn't persuaded; she attempted no conquest of Guiana. But Raleigh never lost his dream. In James I's reign, he was imprisoned (probably unfairly) for plotting against the King. In 1616 he persuaded James to release him so he could search once more for Guiana's gold. In Guiana, Raleigh sent his servant, Keymis, to look for gold. But he found none, and during a fight with the Spaniards,

Right: The ruins of Machupicchu, in Peru. The Incas, or 'people of the sun', were sun worshippers and lived in great cities like this. Spanish conquistadores, led by Pizarro, defeated the Incas in 1531–3.

Left: Raleigh reported that he treated the Indians well, unlike the Spaniards. 'I suffered not any man to take from any of the Indians so much as a potato root without compensation.' But this engraving shows Raleigh on his quest, with his Indian bearers receiving harsh treatment.

Raleigh's son was killed. Raleigh wrote to his wife: 'I never knew what sorrow meant till now'. He told Keymis 'that he had undone me', whereupon Keymis killed himself.

James wanted peace with Spain, and Raleigh knew that he would be executed if he fought any Spaniards. Despite this, he returned to England, where he was beheaded. His vision of 'that great and golden city which the Spaniards call El Dorado' had lured him to destruction.

1 What were Raleigh's aims when he visited Guiana in 1595?

2 Do you think Manoa really existed? Give your reasons.

3 a) How did Raleigh treat the Indians in Trinidad and Guiana. Why do you think this was? b) Did Raleigh mislead the Indians? Give reasons for your answer.

4 a) What is meant by a place 'so far off as the sun slept'? b) Why might Raleigh identify the Epuremei with the 'Inca' people of El Dorado?

8

The lure of the East

Above: Martin Frobisher in 1577.

After 1550, English explorers and merchants were active in many different parts of the world. England's main trade, the cloth trade with Antwerp, was badly disrupted when Protestant rebels in the Netherlands fought against Spanish control (1566–1609). English merchants now needed direct trade with other countries. They successfully developed trade with North Africa, especially Morocco, and with Turkey. But the lure of Asia and its riches still remained strong.

The search for a north-west passage

Englishmen knew that they could reach Asia either by travelling east, or by travelling west. English explorers who travelled west in search of Asia had to go either south of America (like Drake), or north of it. Martin Frobisher and John Davis both tried to find a north-west passage to Asia, a route round the north west of America.

Frobisher's 'Straits'

Frobisher, a tough, experienced sailor, led three north-west expeditions in 1576, 1577 and 1578. In 1576 he reached Baffin Island (see map pages 2–3). George Best, one of his companions, said that Frobisher found

66 a great passage, dividing as it were two continents asunder and so entered the same and passed about fifty leagues therein. And that land upon his right hand as he sailed westwards he judged to be Asia, and America lieth upon the left hand. This place he named 'Frobisher's Straits'. 99

Frobisher thought he'd found the north-west passage to China (see map, below). But instead of a strait, a water passage linking sea to sea, he'd discovered a bay, surrounded on three sides by land. We now call this Frobisher Bay.

On his next two voyages, Frobisher did a bit more exploring, but not much. He encountered Eskimos who tried to prevent him landing. Dionyse Settle, a gentleman who accompanied Frobisher, described the Eskimos:

66 They eat their meat all raw. For lack of water they will eat ice that is hard frozen as pleasantly as we will do sugar candy. Those beasts which they kill, they are both meat, drink, apparel (clothes), houses and almost all their riches. Their houses are tents made of seal skins. Their weapons are bows, arrows, darts, and slings. 99

But Frobisher's main interest was not in the Eskimos. He wanted to mine some black rock he hoped would contain gold. It didn't!

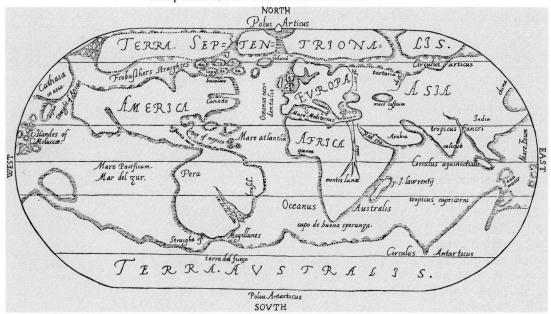

Left: This is a map published by George Best in 1578 in his account of Frobisher's voyages. It illustrates Frobisher's belief in the north-west passage. This runs via 'Frobisher's Straits' north-west round America and then to China through the 'Straits of Anian', which sixteenth century mapmakers thought divided America from Asia. Frobisher expected the route to be short and easy. But arctic ice makes all north-west routes very difficult.

The Davis Strait

Davis, an expert navigator, made three voyages (in 1585, 1586, and 1587), also seeking Asia by a north-west route. He described them in a book published in 1591. In 1585 he found the strait later named 'Davis Strait' after him (see map, pages 2–3).

66 We shaped our course west north-west thinking thereby to pass for China. But in the latitude of 66 degrees we fell with another shore (Baffin Island), and there found another passage directly west (Cumberland Sound) which we supposed to be our hoped Strait. We entered into the same 30 or 40 leagues. 99

On his return home, Davis reported that there was undoubtedly a north-west passage that was usually free of ice.

Davis met some Greenland Eskimos in 1585. He judged them to be 'void of double dealing and easy to be brought to civilization.' But in 1586 he found them 'marvellous thievish, especially for iron.' However, he told his men not to harm them, for he found the Eskimos' inability to resist stealing 'an occasion of laughter.'

In 1587, he explored more of Davis Strait. But if he had gone much further north west, he would soon have been in great trouble from Arctic ice. Not till 1850 did a ship manage to navigate the north-west passage. Even today, ships find it hard to force a way through the ice to Bering Strait.

The south-east route to the Indies

After Davis, interest in the north-west faded until the seventeenth century. Instead, a group of English merchants in the 1590s planned to reach the East Indies by sailing south east, round Africa. This was Portugal's route, but by now Portugal was not strong enough to stop foreigners from using it. Elizabeth did not mind angering Portugal as it had been ruled by England's enemy, Spain, since 1580. (England and Spain were at war 1585–1604.)

James Lancaster's voyage to the East Indies

In 1591–4, James Lancaster followed the Portuguese route to the East. He was backed by London merchants, probably those involved in trade with Turkey. He set off, 'with three tall ships, the *Penelope*, the *Merchant Royal*, and the *Edward Bonaventure*'. Edmund Barker, who sailed with Lancaster, reported that near the Cape of Good Hope:

66 our men being weak and sick (with scurvy) we thought good rather to proceed with two ships well manned than with three evil manned: for we had of sound men but 198. We left behind 50 men with the *Royal Merchant*, which we thought good to send home. 99

Later the *Penelope* was lost. Lancaster battled on in the *Edward*. but:

66 four days after we had a terrible clap of thunder which slew four of our men outright and of 94 men there was not one untouched, some were stricken blind, others bruised in their breasts so that they vomited blood two days after. 99

Several more men were killed by natives near Mozambique. When Lancaster finally reached the East Indies, disease struck.

66 We had left us but 33 men and one boy, of which not past 22 were sound for labour. 99

Despite all these hardships, Lancaster reached home safely.

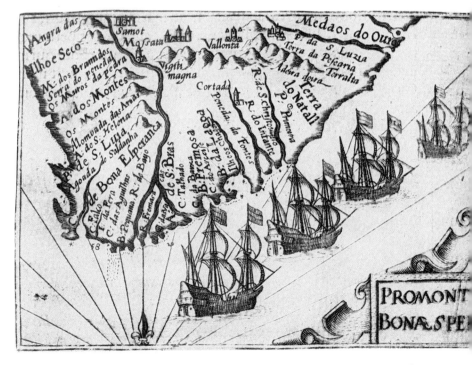

East India Company merchants (or ships) rounding the Cape of Good Hope. From the beginning of the 17th century, Cape Town became an important refreshment station for ships going to and from the East.

The East India Company

Lancaster's voyage was a success. It was not profitable, but it showed that it was possible for English ships to use the south-eastern route to the Indies. English merchants set up the East India Company in 1600 to organize further voyages.

The East India Company was organized as a 'joint-stock' trading company. Joint-stock meant that, instead of each merchant using his own money to pay for a voyage, a group of merchants pooled their funds and paid for voyages jointly. This way, it was easier to afford the long, uncertain journeys to distant parts of the world. A company was also useful because it was 'official' and had more influence than one merchant alone. It could negotiate with local rulers to get permission for English merchants to trade in their ports, and to rule themselves under their own, English, law.

The East India Company had a monopoly of English trade between the Cape of Good Hope and Magellan's Straits. At first it aimed to trade in the East Indies for spices. But the Dutch were powerful in the East Indies now, and their ships attacked English ones. Soon, most English merchants retreated and traded with India instead.

The East India Company wanted to trade with India for its cotton goods. In the early seventeenth century the Mughal Emperor (ruler of India) gave permission for a 'factory', or trading station, to be set up at Surat. Later, the Company was allowed to trade with, and settle in, other Indian ports. The East India Company prospered. It became the wealthiest company in England.

After 1700, local rulers in India broke away from the Emperor's control. There was war and disorder. By now the East India Company had its own soldiers. It began to fight against hostile Indian princes, and also against French attempts to become powerful in India. By 1850 the Company was the main power in India. In 1858 (after a revolt, the 'Indian Mutiny', in 1857) the British government took over the Company's responsibility for ruling India. Queen Victoria became Empress in 1876. The British empire in India did not end till 1947.

India was ruled after 1526 by Mughal emperors like Akbar the Great (1556–1605). He is shown in this seventeenth century Mughal drawing, receiving gifts from people of different nations. The man in European dress is thought to represent King James I of England.

1 a) Why did Englishmen want to find a north-west passage? b) Where did they expect it to run? c) How useful a route is the north-west passage?

2 a) Why do you suppose the Eskimos were 'marvellous thievish' for iron? b) What do you think the Eskimos might have felt about the English visits?

3 a) Why did Lancaster send the *Merchant Royal* home in 1591? b) List the different reasons why Lancaster's men died on the voyage.

4 a) Who were England's main rivals in the East Indies? b) How successful was the English East India Company?

9 A seafaring nation

As a schoolboy in the 1560s, Richard Hakluyt the Younger used to visit his cousin, the elder Richard Hakluyt. The latter, a London lawyer, was already trying to encourage overseas voyages. Hakluyt the Younger wrote that, in his cousin's room,

> I found lying open certain books of Cosmography (the study of the earth's features), with an universal Map: he seeing me somewhat curious began to instruct my ignorance. From the Map he brought me to the Bible, to the Psalm 107, where I read, that they which go down to the sea in ships, and occupy by the great waters, they see the works of the Lord, and his wonders in the deep.

His own enthusiasm for discovery roused, the Younger Hakluyt then tried, through his writing, to inspire others. He collected accounts of English voyages of discovery and published them in a book called *The Principal Navigations, Voyages, ... and Discoveries of the English Nation* (1589). In this, he wrote:

> As in all former ages, the English have been stirrers abroad, and searchers of the remote parts of the world, so in this most famous government of her most excellent Majesty, her subjects through the special assistance, and blessing of God, in searching the most opposite corners and quarters of the world, have excelled all the nations and people of the earth.
>
> (*Principal Navigations*, 1589)

The British Empire

This was a wild exaggeration. But the Tudors did take the first steps towards the later growth of English trade and power overseas. By the eighteenth century Britain had the strongest navy in Europe, and was Europe's leading trading nation. Britain then built up one of the largest overseas empires ever seen.

Britain's empire made her rich and powerful in the nineteenth century. But by the twentieth the expenses and difficulties of running the empire began to outweigh the gains

Britain made from it. Many native peoples now demanded the right to rule themselves. After 1945 Britain gave her colonies independence, though many of them chose to keep close links with Britain by joining a 'Commonwealth of Nations' headed by Queen Elizabeth II.

It is hard to measure the effects of British rule. Some peoples have probably benefitted from a more advanced science and technology, or from firm rule, law and order. Others have suffered from changes made to their agriculture, environment, or way of life. Some cultures have been wiped out. Tudor seamen had no idea, when they first started adventuring overseas, of the consequences their actions would have for future generations.

The Victorians thought the Elizabethans were the first builders of the British empire. This picture, by the Victorian artist, Millais, is called 'The Boyood of Raleigh'. It paints an imaginary scene from Raleigh's childhood. Young Walter sits, wide-eyed, drinking in an old West Country sailor's tales of the sea. Some people would say this shows a 'romantic' view of the past which is probably more imaginative than true to life.

1 a) How did the Younger Hakluyt become interested in overseas discovery? b) What message do you suppose he understood from Psalm 107?

2 Think back over the motives of the adventurers you've studied. List the different motives you find, and show which were the most common.

3 What does Millais' picture of Raleigh make you feel? What does it suggest to you about the Victorian attitude towards Elizabethan seafaring? Do you share this attitude?

Index

Illustration references are shown in heavy type

Dedication For Tony

Acknowledgements
The publishers would like to thank the following for permission to reproduce photographs:

Bodleian Library, Oxford, p. 28 (top); British Library, London, pp. 9 (bottom), 27 (bottom), 29; British Museum, p. 21 (top right, middle, bottom left and right); John Freeman, p. 12 (top and bottom); Freer Gallery, New York, p. 30; Robert Harding Picture Library, pp. 8 (top right), 15, 27 (top); Hutchison Library (John Downman), p. 17 (bottom); Rob Judges, p. 4 (top); Mittet Foto A/S, p. 8 (bottom); Nationalmuseet, Copenhagen, p. 8 (top left); National Portrait Gallery, pp. 14 (top), 23, 26 (top); National Trust Photographic Library (Nick Carter), p. 18; Pepys Library, Magdalene College, Cambridge, p. 13; Plymouth City Museums & Art Gallery Collection, p. 11; Tate Gallery, London, p. 31.

Illustrations by: John Batchelor, p. 24; John Ireland, pp. 7, 10, 14 (bottom), 19, 25 (top), 26 (bottom); Oxford Illustrators, p. 2–3.

Cover illustration: title page of *The Mariners Mirrour*, Lucas J Wagenar, by permission of the Folger Shakespeare Library.

Oxford University Press, Walton Street, Oxford OX2 6DP

Oxford New York Toronto
Delhi Bombay Calcutta Madras Karachi
Petaling Jaya Singapore Hong Kong Tokyo
Nairobi Dar es Salaam Cape Town
Melbourne Auckland

and associated companies in

Berlin Ibadan

Oxford is a trademark of Oxford University Press

© Oxford University Press 1989

ISBN 0 19 913309 3 (limp, non-net)
ISBN 0 19 913350 6 (cased, net)

Typeset by MS Filmsetting Limited, Frome, Somerset
Printed in Hong Kong